Superfast
BOATS

by Mark Dubowski
Consultant: Paul F. Johnston, Washington, D.C.

BEARPORT
PUBLISHING COMPANY, INC.

New York, New York

Credits

Cover, Ken Warby/Ruskin Museum; Title Page, Ken Warby/Ruskin Museum; 4, Ken Warby/Ruskin Museum; 5, Ken Warby/Ruskin Museum; 6-7, Australian Government National Archives of Australia; 8, Bettmann/Corbis; 9, Bettmann/Corbis; 10, Bettmann/Corbis; 11, Hulton Archives/Getty Images; 12-13, Hulton Archives/Getty Images; 14, Michael Brennan/Corbis; 15, Michael Brennan/Corbis; 16, AP Wide World Photos; 17, The Mystic Seaport Museum; 18, The Detroit News; 19, The Detroit News; 20, Nigel Rolstone/Cordaiy Photo Library Ltd./Corbis; 21, Courtesy of Sea Ray; 22-23, Ken Warby/Ruskin Museum; 24-25, Ken Warby/Ruskin Museum; 26, Ken Warby/Ruskin Museum; 27, Ken Warby/Ruskin Museum; 29, Agence France Presse/Getty Images.

Editorial development by Judy Nayer
Design and Production by Paula Jo Smith

Special thanks to Ken Warby

Library of Congress Cataloging-in-Publication Data
Dubowski, Mark.
  Superfast boats / by Mark Dubowski ; consultant: Paul Johnston.
    p. cm.–(Ultimate speed)
  Includes bibliographical references and index.
  ISBN 1-59716-079-2 (library binding) — ISBN 1-59716-116-0 (pbk.)
  1. Jet boats. 2. Motorboat racing. I. Title. II. Series.

  VM348.5.D83 2006
  797.1'4–dc22
                        2005009751

For more information, write to Bearport Publishing Company, Inc., 101 Fifth Avenue, Suite 6R, New York, New York 10003. Printed in the United States of America.

1 2 3 4 5 6 7 8 9 10

CONTENTS

The Fastest Man Alive

Ken Warby seemed like an **average** person. He lived in a house in Cincinnati, Ohio, where he built things in his garage. One of his projects was a new boat called the *Aussie Spirit*. Warby had named it after the country where he was born—Australia.

Ken Warby is the first person to ever design, build, and drive a boat that broke the world water-speed record.

Ken Warby

The *Aussie Spirit* wasn't Ken Warby's first homemade boat. Back in 1978, Warby was in Australia, taking his boat the *Spirit of Australia* for a ride. It was then that the world found out there was nothing average about Ken Warby. On that day, he became the water world's "fastest man alive."

For the world-record run, Ken Warby took his boat to Blowering Dam, in New South Wales, Australia.

The World's Most Dangerous Sport

Ken Warby's *Spirit of Australia* was powered by a 6,000-**horsepower** turbojet. This engine was made for fighter planes. Warby knew that putting this engine on a boat was asking for trouble. At top speed, it would be hard to keep the boat from skipping off the water and flying—or even exploding. If Warby was going to break the world speed record for powerboats, however, he had to use this engine.

Ken Warby and his boat, the *Spirit of Australia*, in 1979

Top-speed boat racing has been called the most dangerous sport in the world. Sadly, many people who get into the record books don't live very long.

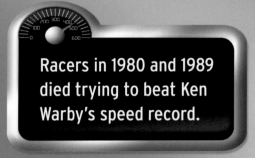

Racers in 1980 and 1989 died trying to beat Ken Warby's speed record.

EYEWITNESS NEWS

SPEEDO.

SPIRIT OF AUSTRALIA

Seven Speed Records in a Row

For years, the fastest man on water was Donald Campbell, from England. His boat was an early hydroplane, a type of **craft** that skims the water's surface. He called it *Bluebird K7*.

The first time Campbell broke the speed record for watercraft was in 1955. Over the next 12 years, he broke his own speed record six more times.

Campbell and the *Bluebird* in 1955

In 1967, Campbell was at a five-mile-long (8 km) lake in England. There was no wind and the water was as smooth as glass. Campbell climbed into the **cockpit** of the *Bluebird K7*, ready to set another world record.

Donald Campbell celebrates after breaking the world water-speed record in 1955.

Donald Campbell's father, Malcolm, was a famous car and boat racer. Malcolm broke the water-speed record four times by the time Donald was 18 years old.

Another Record

Campbell took off for the other end of the lake. He wore a radio microphone. The *Bluebird* hit 297 miles per hour (478 kph). He had gone 21 miles per hour (34 kph) faster than the old record. The race was not over, however.

Donald Campbell's race car

Donald Campbell raced cars as well as boats. In 1964, he became the first person to hold speed records for both land and water in the same year.

Many top-speed races have a "down and back" rule. The racer must first go from start to finish. Then the racer must turn around and return to the starting line. The speeds for both runs are added together and divided by two to get an average. That number is the **official** speed.

Donald Campbell just before he tried to set a new water-speed record on January 4, 1967

300 Miles Per Hour

On the way back to the starting line, Campbell hit almost 300 miles per hour (483 kph). Then he ran into trouble. The *Bluebird* slammed over the ripples made by the boat's own **wake**. The boat's **vibrations** made Campbell's eyes tremble. It was hard to see.

Donald Campbell runs into trouble as he races across the water in the *Bluebird*.

Campbell reported trouble over the radio. "I can't see much," he shouted, "and the water is very bad."

Campbell knew he had to lower the **throttle** and slow the boat down. "I have to draw back," he said. Unfortunately, he never got the chance.

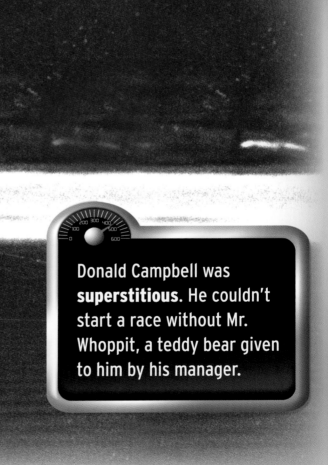

Donald Campbell was **superstitious**. He couldn't start a race without Mr. Whoppit, a teddy bear given to him by his manager.

A Tragic End

The *Bluebird* hit a rough patch of water and lifted off. It did something racers call a barrel roll. The boat flipped end over end above the surface of the water.

Campbell's voice came over the radio. "I've gone . . ." he said, "oh . . . ." Those were his last words.

A barrel roll accident can land a boat upside down.

The *Bluebird* was going almost 300 miles per hour (483 kph) when it made a nosedive back onto the water. At that speed, hitting the water was like hitting a brick wall. The *Bluebird* broke up. Campbell died on **impact**.

The *Bluebird* remained at the bottom of the lake, untouched, for 34 years.

Boating Meets Flying

Years before Campbell was setting records, Garfield "Gar" Arthur Wood was building and racing superfast boats. In 1917, Gar had won the first of five Gold Cup medals for powerboat racing. He thought the only way to go faster was to use a different kind of engine. So he put a Curtiss 12 airplane engine in his boat, the *Miss Detroit III* (3).

Gar was the first person to power a boat using an airplane engine.

Garfield "Gar" Wood

People thought Gar's idea would never work. Powerboating is a rough ride. Airplane engines have delicate parts. Gar showed people they were wrong. The engine worked well and the *Miss Detroit III* won the Gold Cup that same year.

Miss Detriot III at the Gold Cup Races in 1918

Car-Engine Boat

When Gar put an airplane engine in the *Miss Detroit III*, he was just getting started. In 1921, he built a large boat called the *Gar Jr., II* (2). Gar got a lot of attention when he raced the boat against a train from Miami to New York. He beat the train by 12 minutes. The U.S. Navy used Gar's ideas to design a famous fighter craft called the PT boat.

Gar Jr., II

In 1932, Gar broke the world record for motorboat speed when he drove the *Miss America X* (10) at speeds over 124 miles per hour (200 kph). The boat was powered by four car engines.

Miss America X

Gar's 1932 water-speed record was almost twice as fast as cars on today's highways.

High-Tech Building

Top-speed powerboats are built for only one reason—to be the fastest. Winning speed records, however, takes two kinds of skills. On the day of the race it takes driving skill. Before that, one has to spend years developing skills in **engineering** and boat building.

At 48 miles per hour (77 kph), the *SeaCat* is one of the fastest ferries in the world.

Every day, the *SeaCat* carries hundreds of people back and forth across the English Channel between England and France.

Many of today's powerboat builders are **high-tech** engineers. They use their knowledge of boats as well as information from other areas in science. For example, ideas from the field of **aerospace** show builders which shapes will cut through air and water the best. Builders also use **computer science** to help run formulas that predict how different designs will work.

A boat being designed on a computer

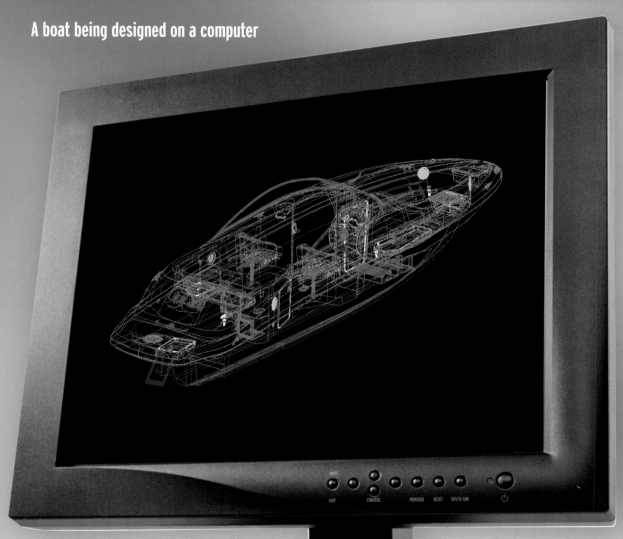

Warby Takes Off

On October 8, 1978, Ken Warby was back in his home country. He was sitting in the cockpit of his homemade powerboat, the *Spirit of Australia*. Through the **visor** of his helmet, he looked across the water. It was wide and flat. A great lake had been made where four rivers came together.

Warby's boat has a wing in back that works like an airplane wing, only backwards. The wing helps to keep the boat from lifting off the water.

300+

It was time to race. Warby hit the throttle. The *Spirit of Australia* roared and took off. Warby blasted across the surface. The water felt like a rocky road, and Warby rattled in the cockpit.

Ken Warby in the *Spirit of Australia* on October 8, 1978

An Amazing Record

As Warby shot across the water, a timekeeper clocked his speed. When it looked like his average speed would be over 277 miles per hour (446 kph), the timekeeper knew Warby would beat Donald Campbell's old record. If Warby could finish faster than 289 miles per hour (465 kph) he would beat his own world record, set the year before.

When the race was over, Warby had set a new world water-speed record. His official speed was 317.6 miles per hour (511 kph).

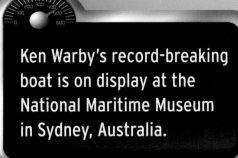

Ken Warby's record-breaking boat is on display at the National Maritime Museum in Sydney, Australia.

The Challengers

Ken Warby's world record got the attention of racers everywhere. Beating it has become their goal. With the help of high-tech engineers, some boat builders think they have a chance. Warby, however, disagrees.

Ken Warby tested his new boat, the *Aussie Spirit*, in January 2005.

Warby can think of only one person who might be able to break the world record. That person is testing a brand-new boat called the *Aussie Spirit*. The driver's name is Ken Warby!

Ken Warby's new boat, the *Aussie Spirit*, has 50 percent more power than his record-breaking *Spirit of Australia*.

Aussie Spirit

JUST THE FACTS More About Superfast Boats

- The first Gold Cup race took place in 1904 on the Hudson River in New York City. The winning boat used a 110-horsepower engine and averaged over 23 miles per hour (37 kph).

- Boat racing superstar Garfield "Gar" Arthur Wood was named after two U.S. Presidents, James Garfield (1831–1881) and Chester Arthur (1829–1886).

- Powerboat racing is so dangerous that rescue teams follow the race from above in helicopters. In case of a crash, the rescue team throws down a line to the racers and gets them out of the water.

- Powerboat engines are so noisy that it is hard for racers to hear. To talk to one another or crew members, the racers use walkie-talkies inside their helmets.

TIMELINE

This timeline shows some important events in the history of superfast boats.

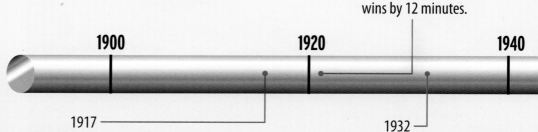

1921
Gar races his boat *Gar Jr., II* against a train from Miami to New York and wins by 12 minutes.

1900   **1920**   **1940**

1917
Gar Wood wins his first Gold Cup medal for powerboat racing and builds the first boat powered by an airplane engine, *Miss Detroit III*.

1932
Gar breaks the world record for speed on water by going over 124 miles per hour (200 kph) in the *Miss America X*.

- Ocean racing yachts speed around the world in the Whitbread Round the World Race. The race takes eight months and the yachts race 31,600 miles (50,855 km).

- The longest race on Earth for one person is the Around Alone, a 27,000-mile (43,452-km) boat race around the world.

Ken Warby and the _Spirit of Australia_ at the Australian National Maritime Museum

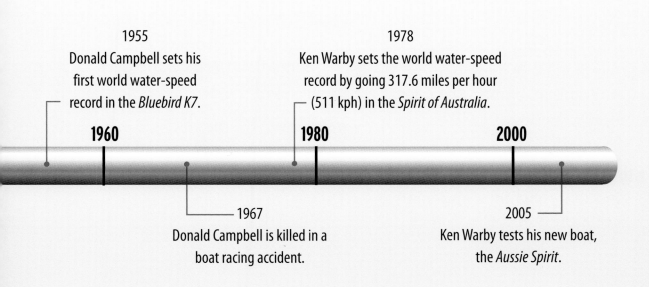

1955
Donald Campbell sets his first world water-speed record in the _Bluebird K7_.

1978
Ken Warby sets the world water-speed record by going 317.6 miles per hour (511 kph) in the _Spirit of Australia_.

1960

1980

2000

1967
Donald Campbell is killed in a boat racing accident.

2005
Ken Warby tests his new boat, the _Aussie Spirit_.

GLOSSARY

aerospace (AIR-oh-spayss) the science of jet flight and space travel

average (AV-uh-rij) ordinary; the number gotten after adding two or more figures, and then dividing that sum by the number of figures added

cockpit (KOK-*pit*) the place where the pilot sits

computer science (kuhm-PYOO-tur SYE-uhnss) the study and use of computers

craft (KRAFT) a vehicle such as a boat, ship, airplane, or spaceship

engineering (en-juh-NIHR-ing) the field of designing and building machines, vehicles, roads, bridges, or other structures

high-tech (hye-TEK) using very modern machines, especially computers and electronics

horsepower (HORSS-*pou*-uhr) a unit for measuring an engine's power

impact (IM-pakt) the striking of one thing against another

official (uh-FISH-uhl) according to the rules

superstitious (*soo*-pur-STI-shuhs) believing something based on the fear of the unknown

throttle (THROT-uhl) a valve in a vehicle's engine that controls the flow of fuel or air

vibrations (vye-BRAY-shunz) quick back-and-forth shaking

visor (VYE-zur) the moveable shield on the front of a helmet that protects the eyes and upper face

wake (WAYK) the track of waves that is left behind a boat moving in the water

BIBLIOGRAPHY

www.javelins.org
www.kenwarby.com
www.powerboatmagazine.com

READ MORE

Andersen, T. J. *Power Boat Racing.* Englewood Cliffs, NJ: Silver Burdett Press (1988).

Bullard, Lisa. *Powerboats.* Minneapolis, MN: Lerner Publications (2004).

Demarest, Chris L. *Mayday! Mayday! A Coast Guard Rescue.* New York: Margaret K. McElderry Books (2004).

Graham, Ian. *Boats.* Austin, TX: Steck-Vaughn Publishing (1998).

Kentley, Eric. *Eyewitness: Boat.* New York: Dorling Kindersley Publishing (2000).

Savage, Jeff. *Hydroplane Boats.* Mankato, MN: Capstone Press (2004).

LEARN MORE ONLINE

Visit these Web sites to learn more about superfast boats:

www.abm.org/Collection/Gold_cup.htm
www.americascup.com
www.unlimitedlights.org

INDEX

ABOUT THE AUTHOR

Mark Dubowski is the author/illustrator of many books for young readers. He lives in North Carolina, where he enjoys scuba diving the many shipwrecks off the "Graveyard of the Atlantic" coast.